The Great Western STEAM UP

Carson City, Nevada

July 1-4 2022

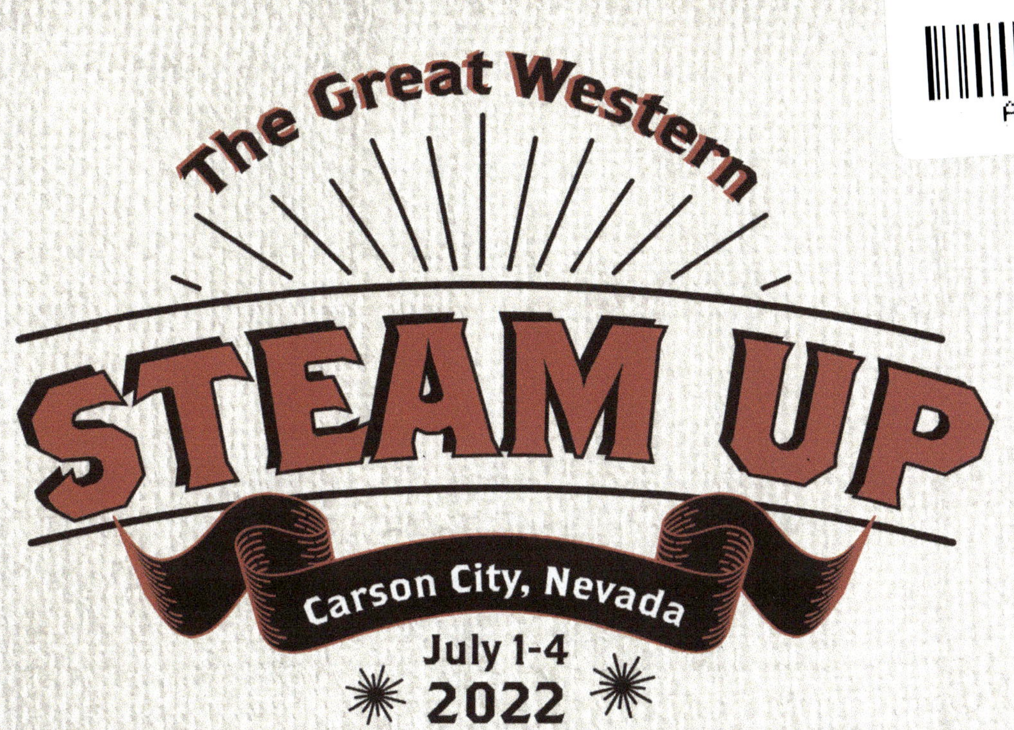

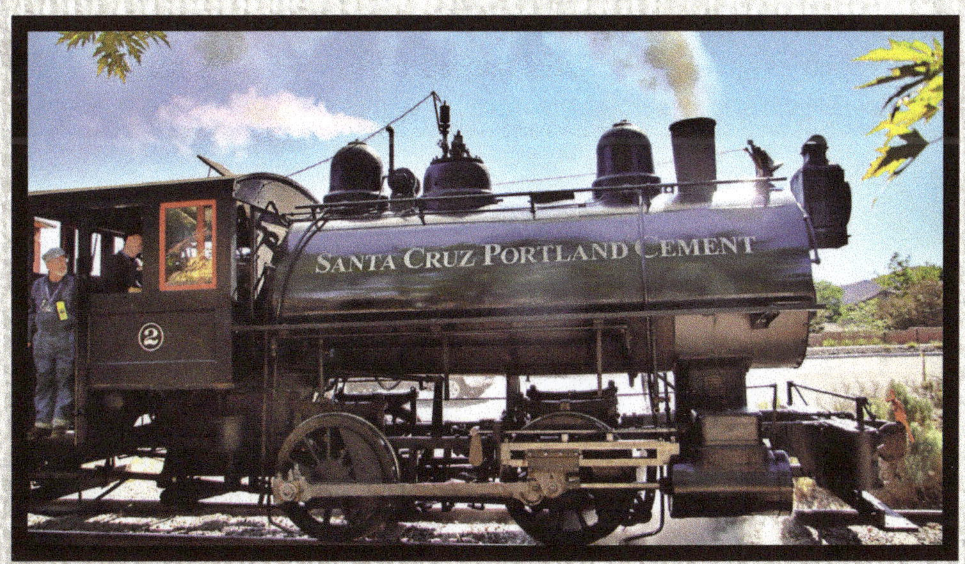

Written and Photographed by Julie Michler

ISBN:978-1-938814-44-0

DEDICATION

This book is dedicated to my father, Otto C. Michler
who enjoyed building and playing with my
brothers and myself as children with toy trains.

A Brief History of the Virginia and Truckee Railroad

The Virginia and Truckee shines as the most famous of all short line railways. Built by the "Bank Crowd" in order to transport the ore from their mines around Virginia City, to their quartz mills on the Carson River. They purchased the finest rolling stock and locomotives money could buy. While the "Big Bonanza" lasted, train movements during the 1870's show a parade of passengers, supplies, ore and bullion. The line was extended to Reno to connect with the Transcontinental Railroad.

When the boom times began to turn to "bust" (late 1870's) the "Bank Crowd" built a narrow gauge railroad called Carson & Colorado Railroad connecting from Mound House to Keeler to tap the mining areas to the south. The line was unfortunately sold before the Tonopah Gold Rush.

The V&T learned to survive the hard times too. When the Comstock mines played out and the mills along the Carson River began to close down the V&T built a fifteen mile branch from Carson City to Minden to tap the agricultural area to the south.

Hollywood discovered the V&T in the late 1930's and a few locomotives and cars began to leave the property for new careers on the silver screen. This desire on the studio's part was a major factor in the preservation of the line's historic rolling stock and engines.

But the handwriting was on the wall. The V&T was loosing a great deal of money. The pressures of the post World War II economy did not allow for such a luxury railroad.

V&T operations to Virginia City were suspended in 1938 and the track was taken up in 1941. In 1950 the ten wheeler #27 pulled the final train into Reno and the V&T was officially abandoned. But this is not the end of the story as her eighty-odd years of old records, as well as many of her historic cars and locomotives still survive today. All locomotives that were present at the steam up were under steam and operational except *Lyon #1*", "*Genoa #12*", "*J.W. Bowker #21*" and non V&T "*Dardanelle and Russellville* Railroad #8" and "*Joe Douglas #21*" engines.

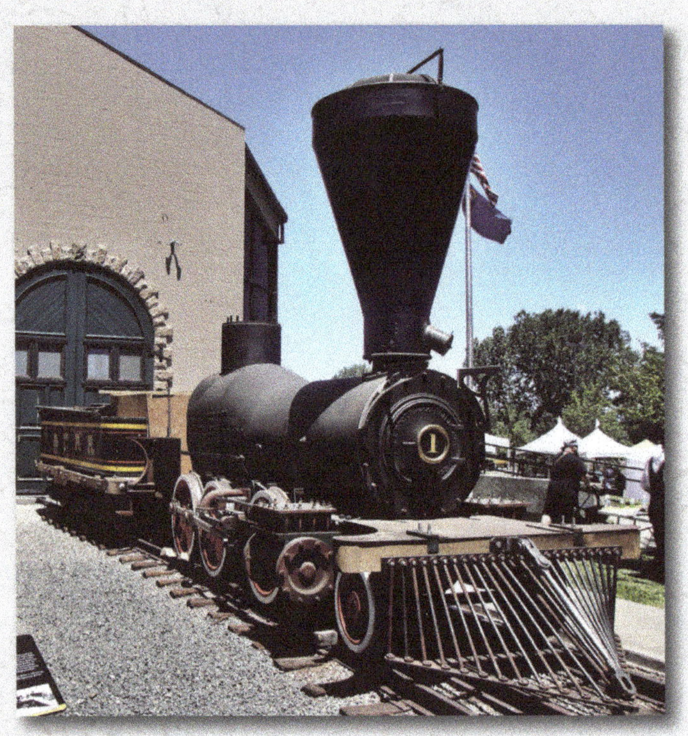

#1 *Lyon*   V&T Locomotive

- 2-6-0   H. J. Booth and Co., San Francisco Builder
- Standard Gauge
- Built 1869 Retired 1887
- Slowly dismantled for parts
- She is being constructed as a replica of the original V&T #1, Carson City, NV

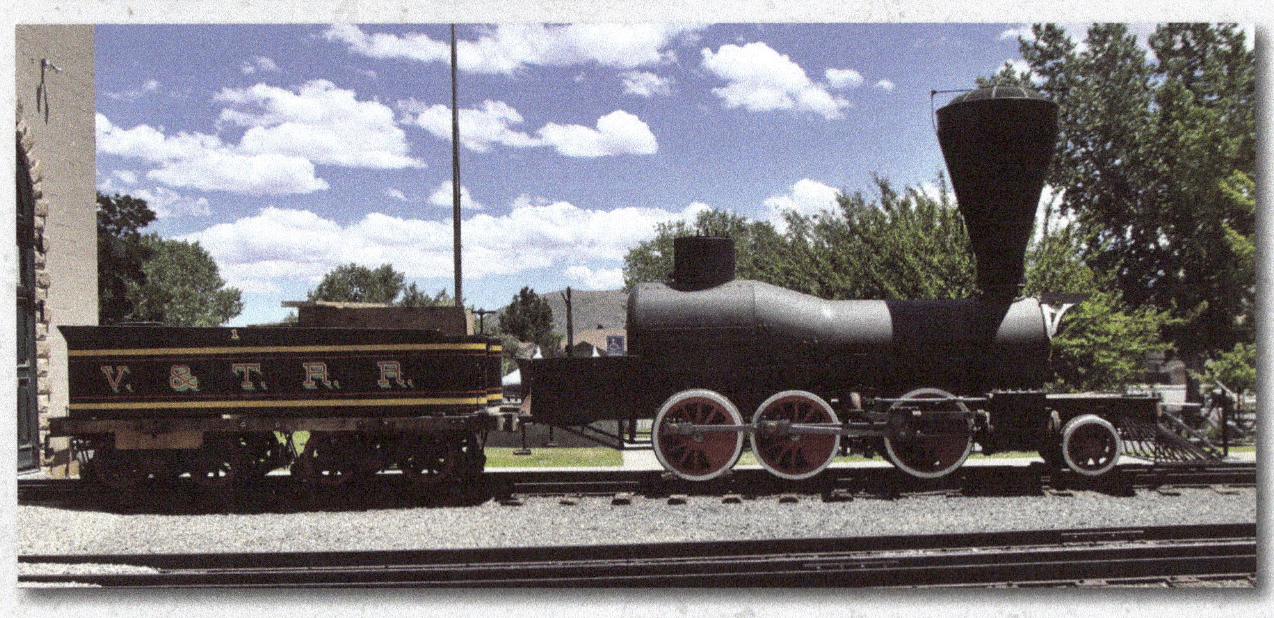

#11 *Reno*   V&T Locomotive

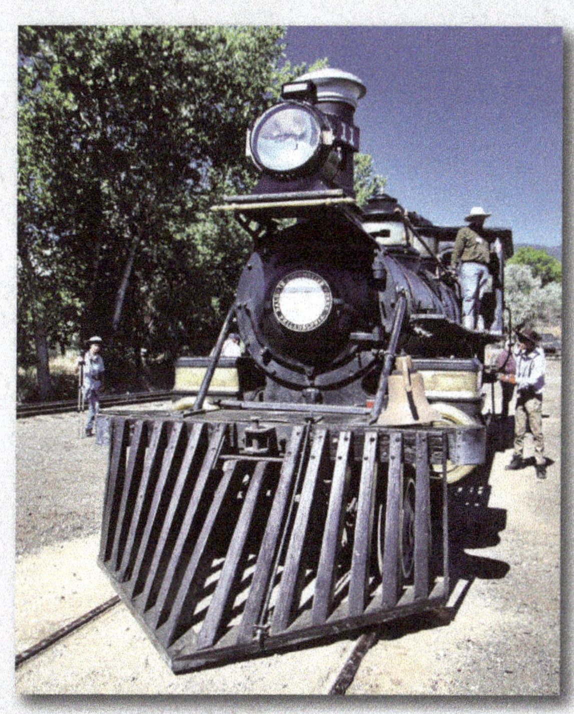

- 4-4-0   Baldwin Locomotive Works of Philadelphia Builder
- Standard Gauge
- Built 1872 Sold to MGM Studios 1945
- Sold to Old Tuscon Studios, Arizona 1970
- Was damaged in a studio fire 1995
- Purchased by the Virginia & Truckee Railroad Company, Virginia City, NV

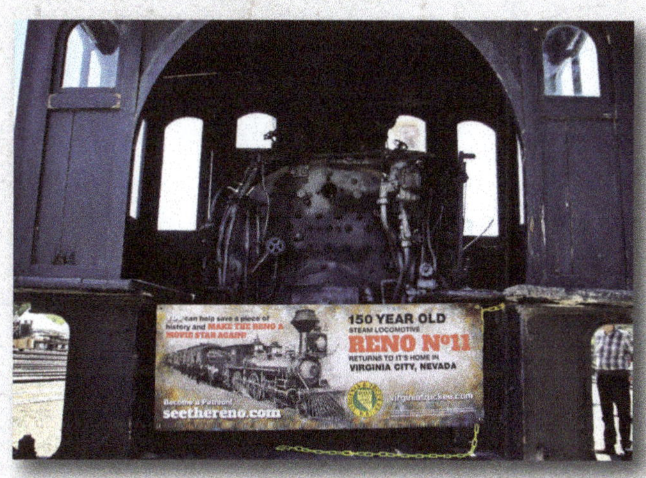

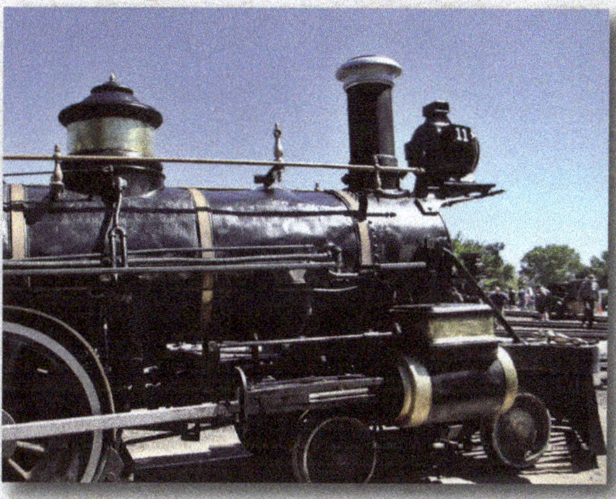

#12 *Genoa*   V&T Locomotive

- 4-4-0   Baldwin Locomotive Works of Philadelphia Builder
- Standard Gauge
- Built 1873 Retired 1908
- She is owned by the California State Museum and is restored to her circa 1902 appearance
- She is currently on a two-year loan to the Nevada State Railroad Museum in Carson City, Nevada

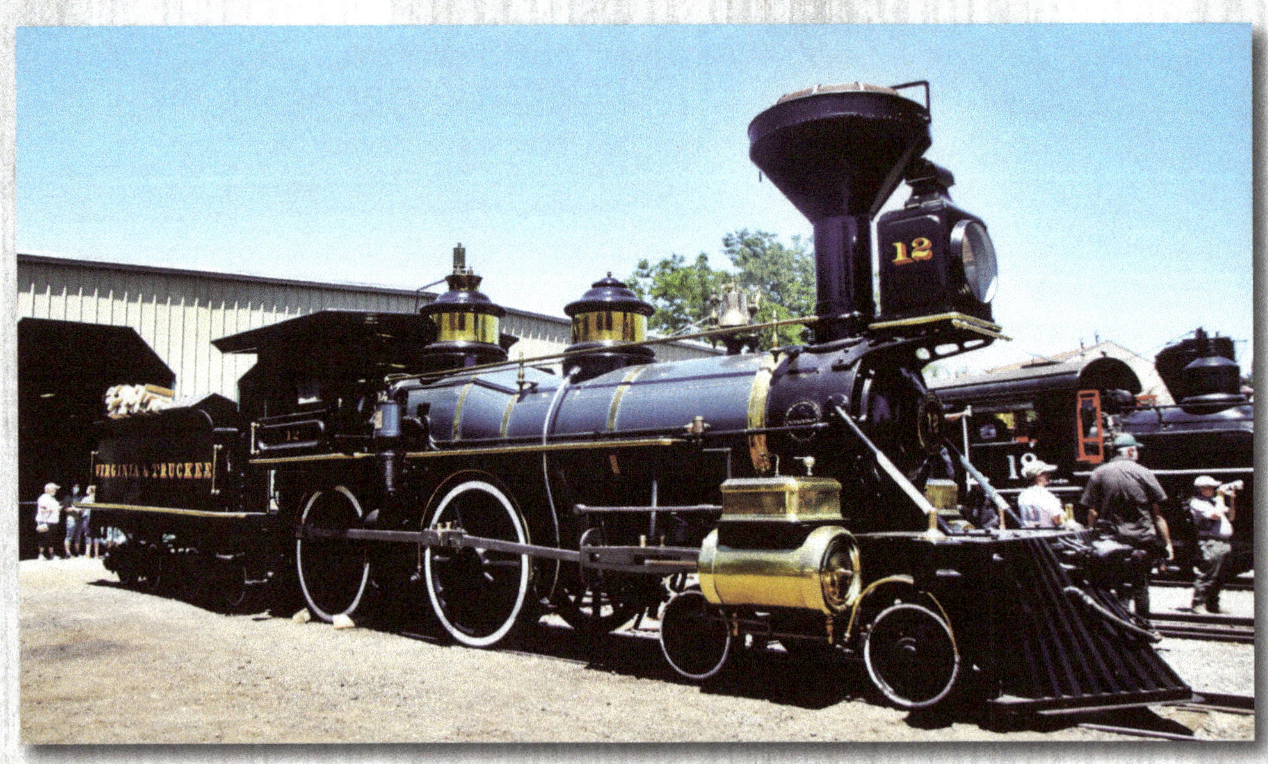

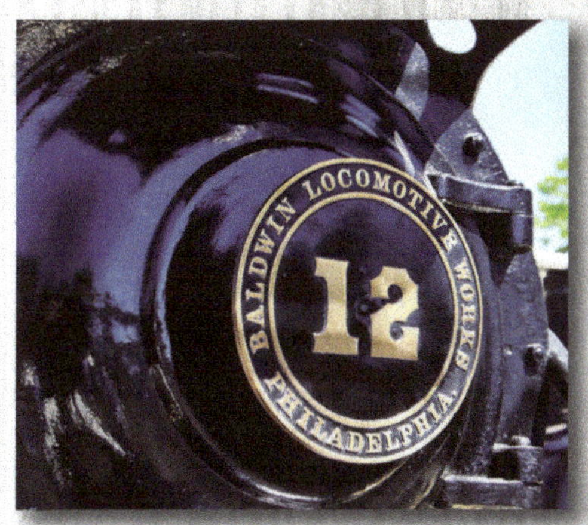
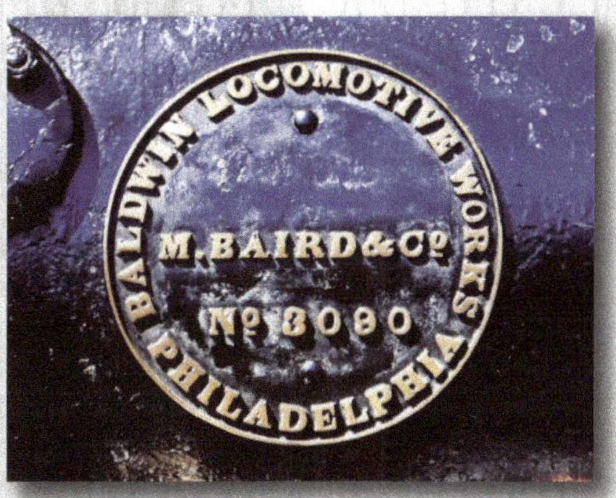
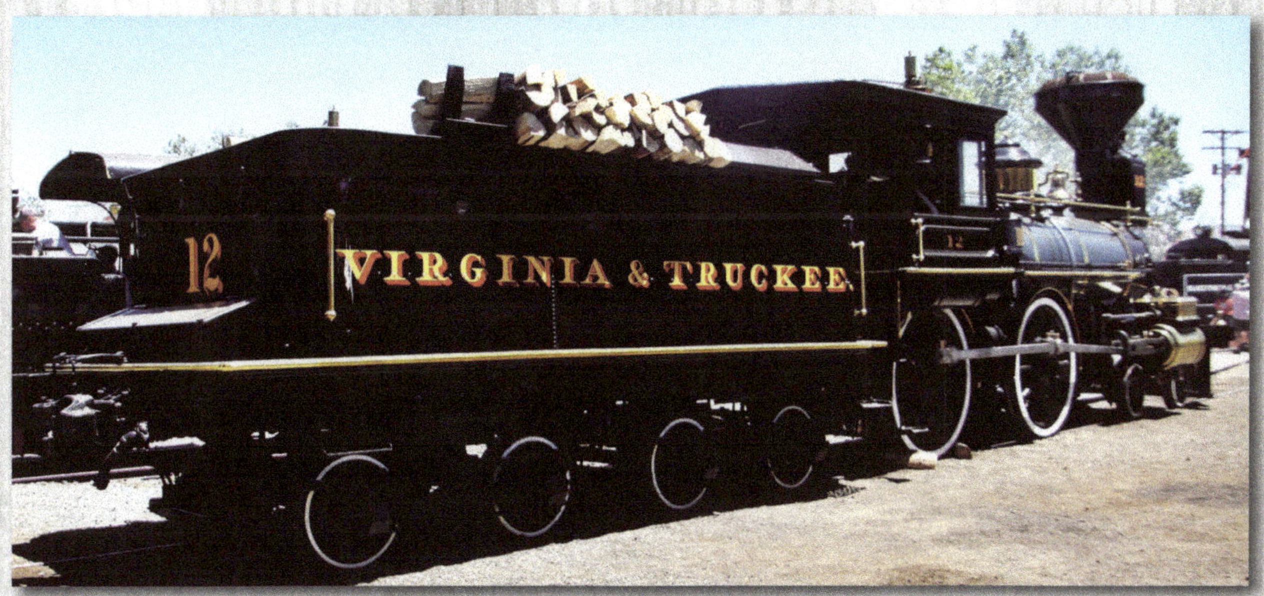

#18 *Dayton*   V&T Locomotive

- 4-4-0   Central Pacific Railroad Builder
- Standard Gauge
- Built 1873
- Sold to Paramount Studios 1938
- Sold to State of Nevada 1974
- She is owned by the Nevada State Railroad Museum in Carson City, Nevada, and was restored to her 1882 appearance at Nevada State Railroad Museum, Carson City, NV
- She is currently on a two-year loan to the California State Railroad Museum in Old Sacramento, California

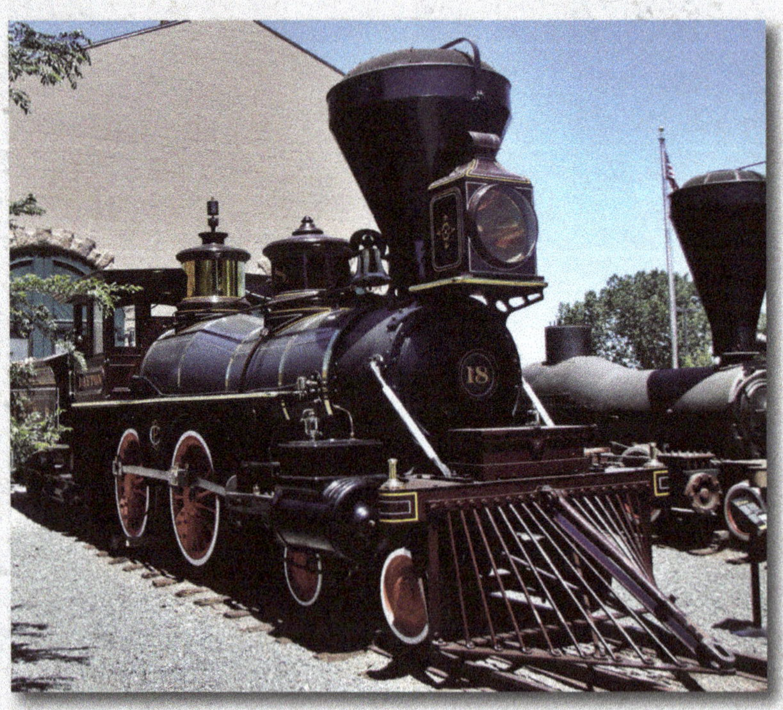

#21 *J. W. Bowker*   V&T Locomotive

- 2-4-0   Baldwin Locomotive Works of Philadelphia Builder
- Standard Gauge
- Built 1875 Retired 1917
- Donated to California State Railroad Museum, Sacramento 1969
- She is owned by the California State Railroad Museum in Old Sacramento, California and is currently on a two-year loan to the Nevada State Railroad Museum in Carson City, Nevada.
- It has been restored to its circa 1875 appearance

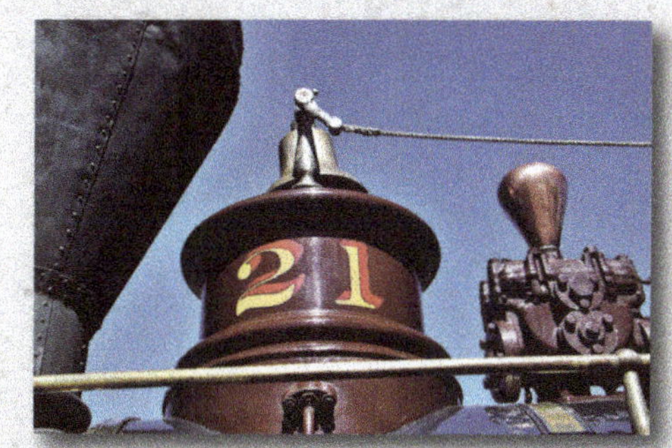

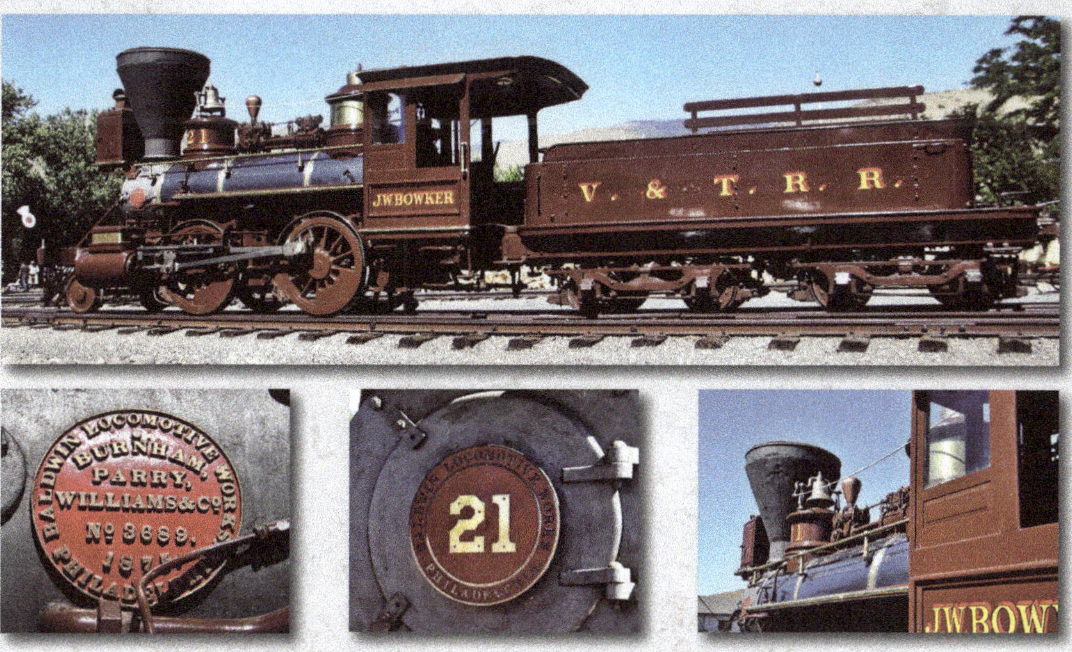

#22 *Inyo*   V&T Locomotive

- 4-4-0   Baldwin Locomotive Works of Philadelphia Builder
- Standard Gauge
- Built 1875 Retired 1926
- Sold to Paramount Studios 1937
- Sold to State of Nevada 1974
- Restored to 1892 appearance and operational 1984

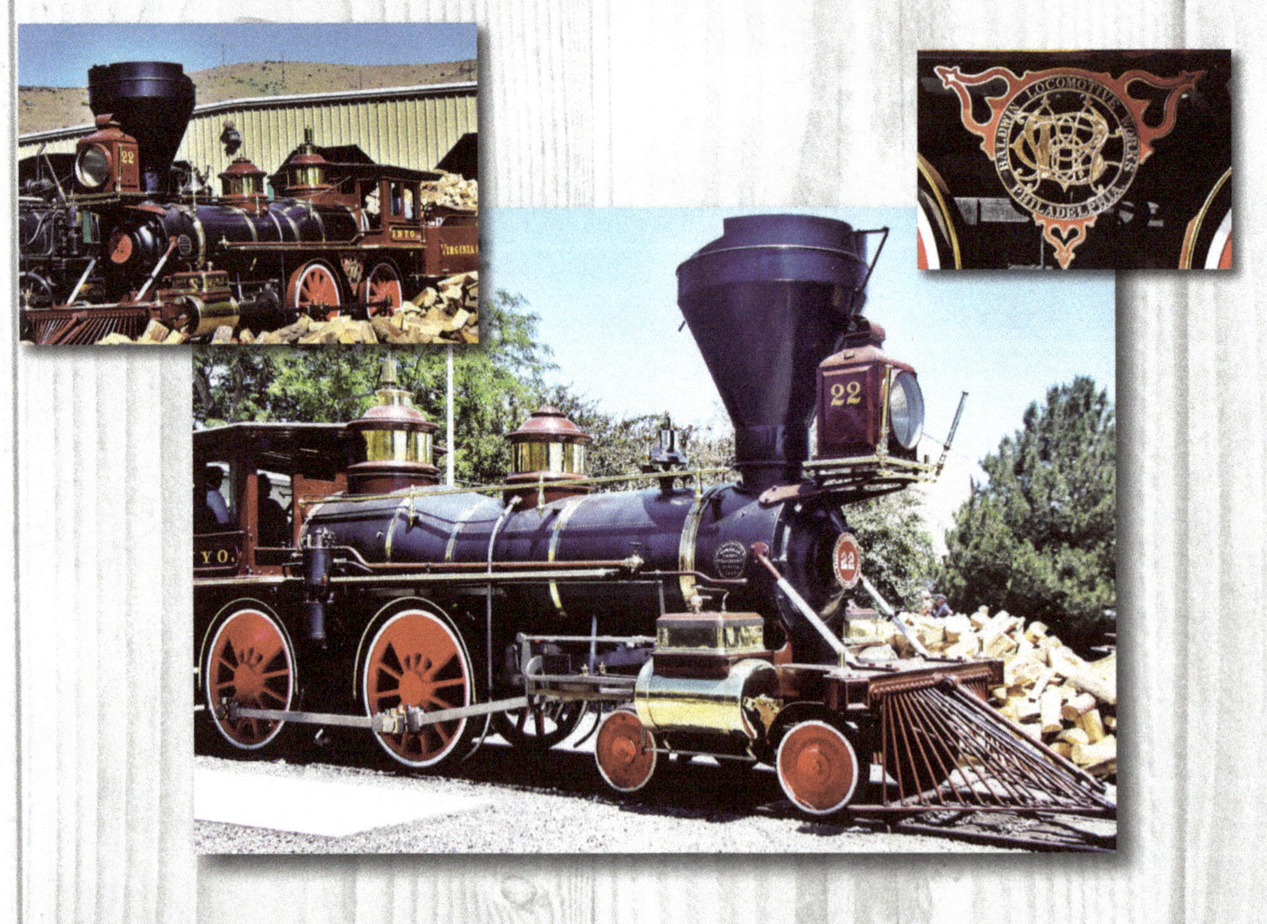

#25 (Second Locomotive)
V&T Locomotive

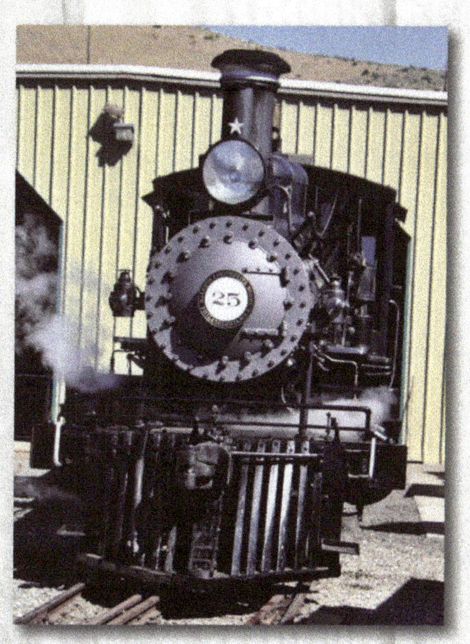

- 4-6-0   Baldwin Locomotive Works of Philadelphia Builder
- Standard Gauge
- Built 1905
- Sold to RKO Studios 1947
- Sold to Nevada State Museum 1971
- Restored to service 1980 at Carson City, NV

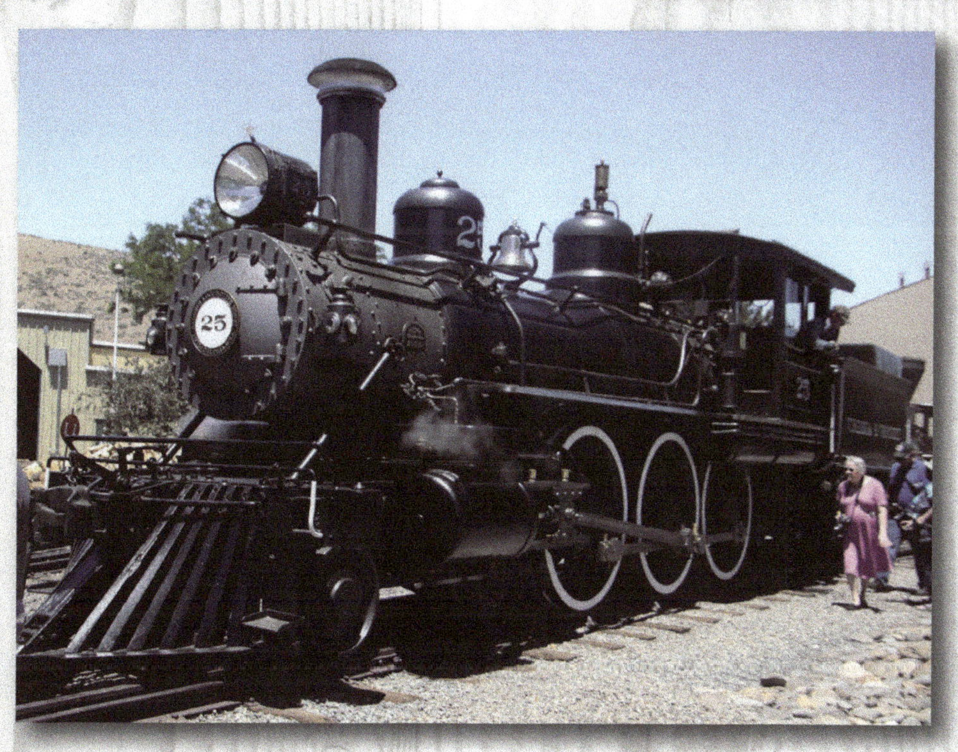

#18 *"Slim Princess"* Carson and Colorado/Southern Pacific Railroad

- 4-6-0   Baldwin Locomotive Works of Philadelphia Builder
- Narrow Gauge
- Built 1911
- Was actually built as Nevada-California-Oregon Locomotiove #12
- Retired 1954
- Sold to Southern Pacific 1928
- Donated to Inyo County, CA 1955
- Restored 2021 for operation

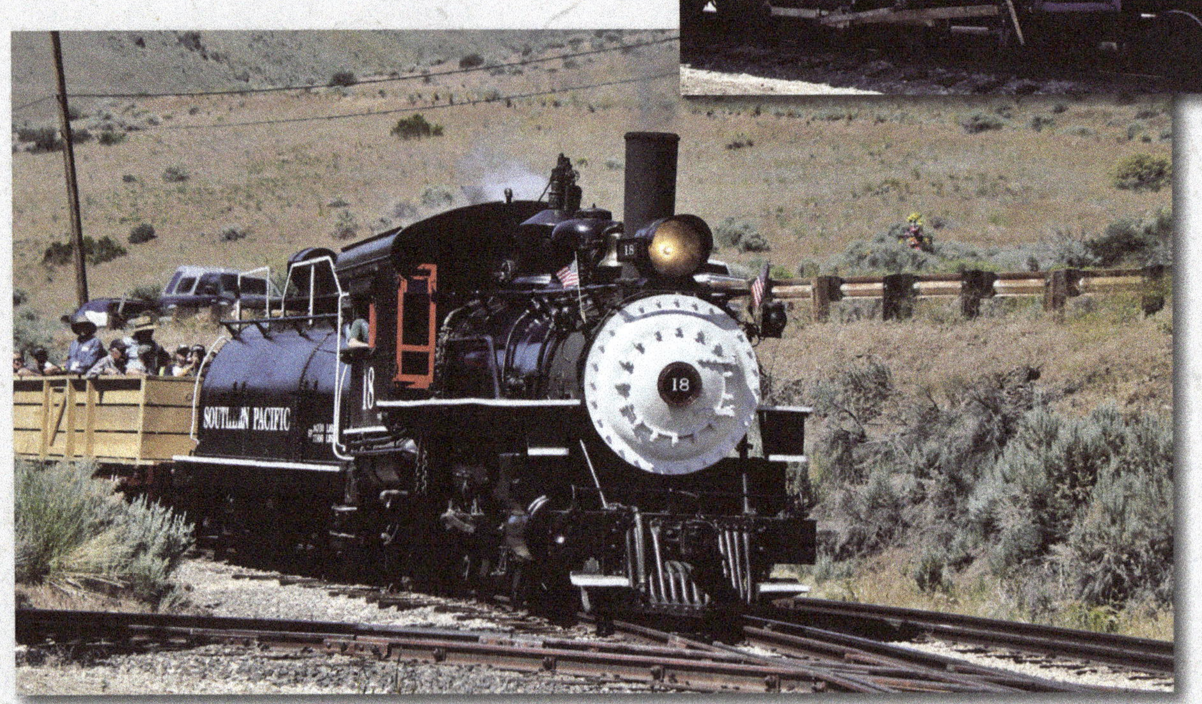

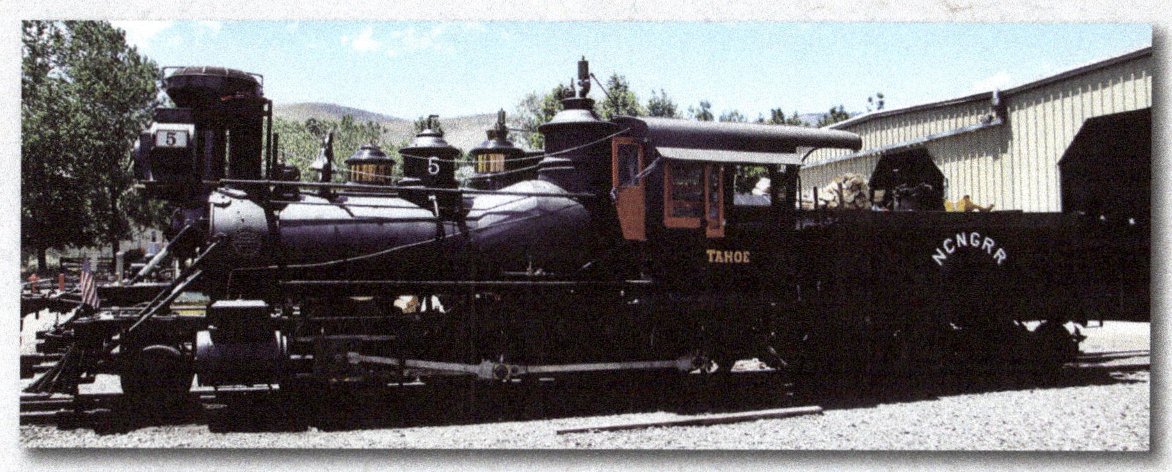

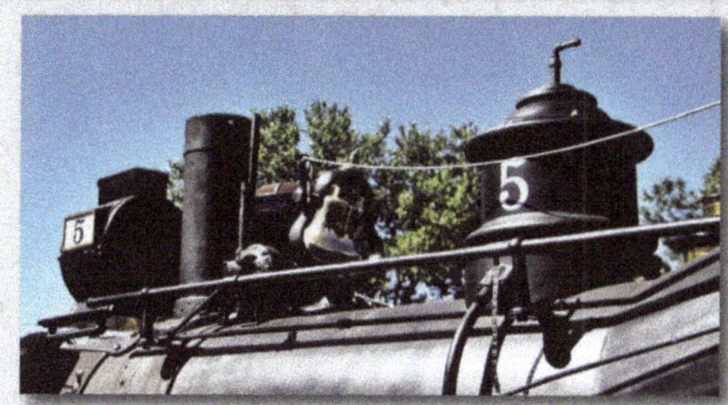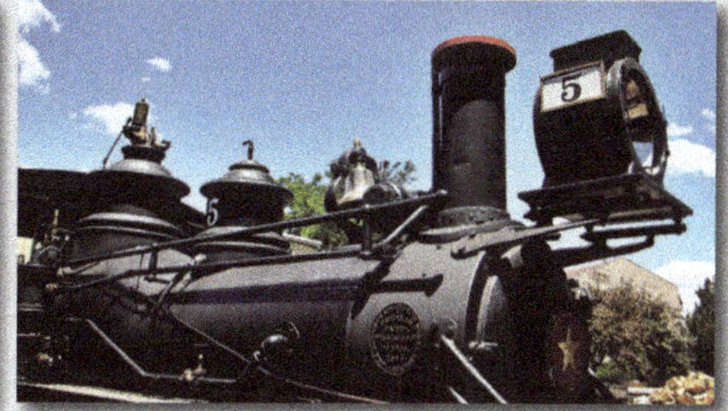

#5 *Tahoe Carson and Tahoe Lumber and Fluming Co.*

- 2-6-0 Baldwin Locomotive Works of Philadelphia Builder
- Narrow Gauge
- Built 1875
- Sold to Nevada County Narrow Gauge Railroad, Grass Valley, CA 1899
- In the movies 1942
- Sold to Nevada County Historical Society, Grass Valley, CA 1985

Glenbrook Carson and Tahoe Lumber & Fluming Co.

- 2-6-0   Baldwin Locomotive Works of Philadelphia Builder
- Narrow Gauge
- Built 1875
- Used by Lake Tahoe Railway and Transportation Co. 1898
- Sold to Nevada State Museum, Carson City, NV 1943

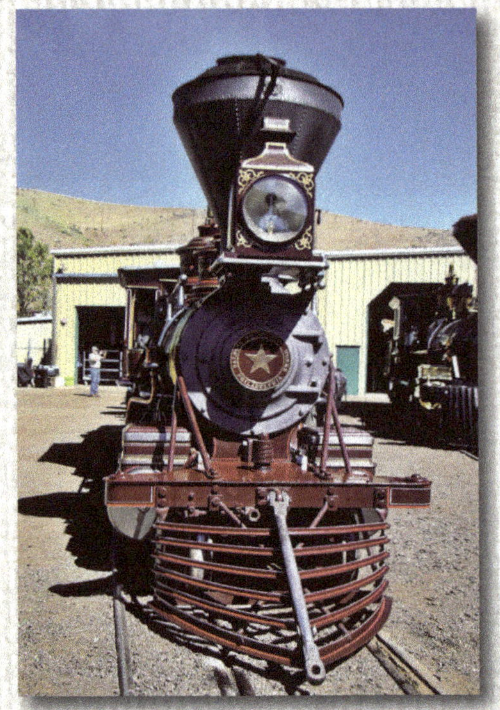

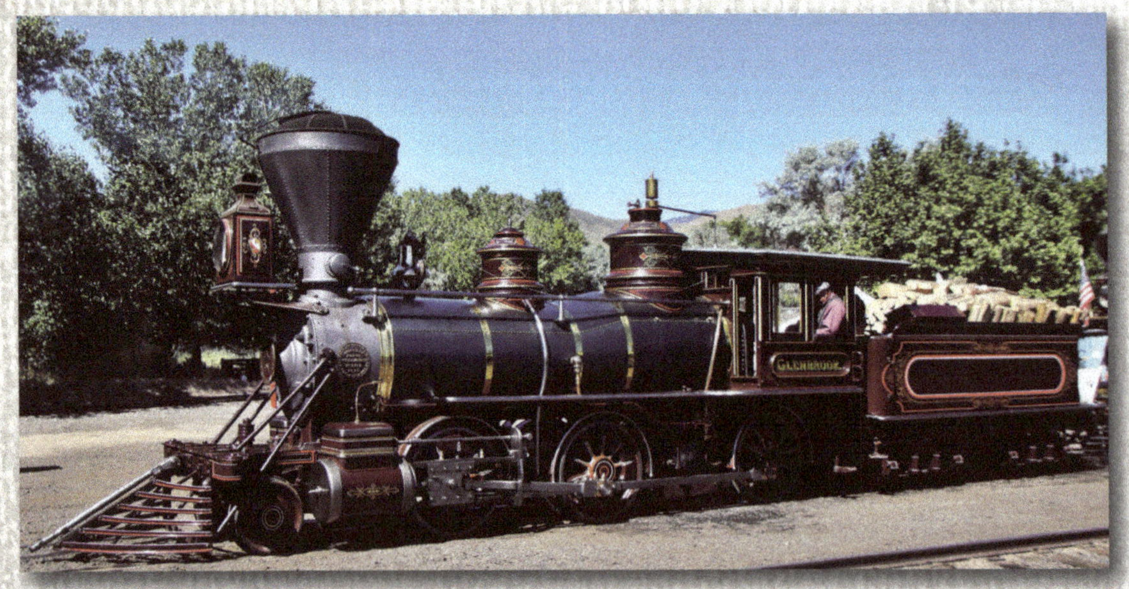

Joe Douglass   Dayton, Sutro & Carson Valley Railroad

- 0-4-2   H. K. Porter and Co., Pittsburgh, PA Builder
- Narrow Gauge
- Built 1882
- Used by the Birdshall/Douglass Mill, in Dayton, NV
- Sold to Nevada State Railroad Museum, Carson City, NV 1994

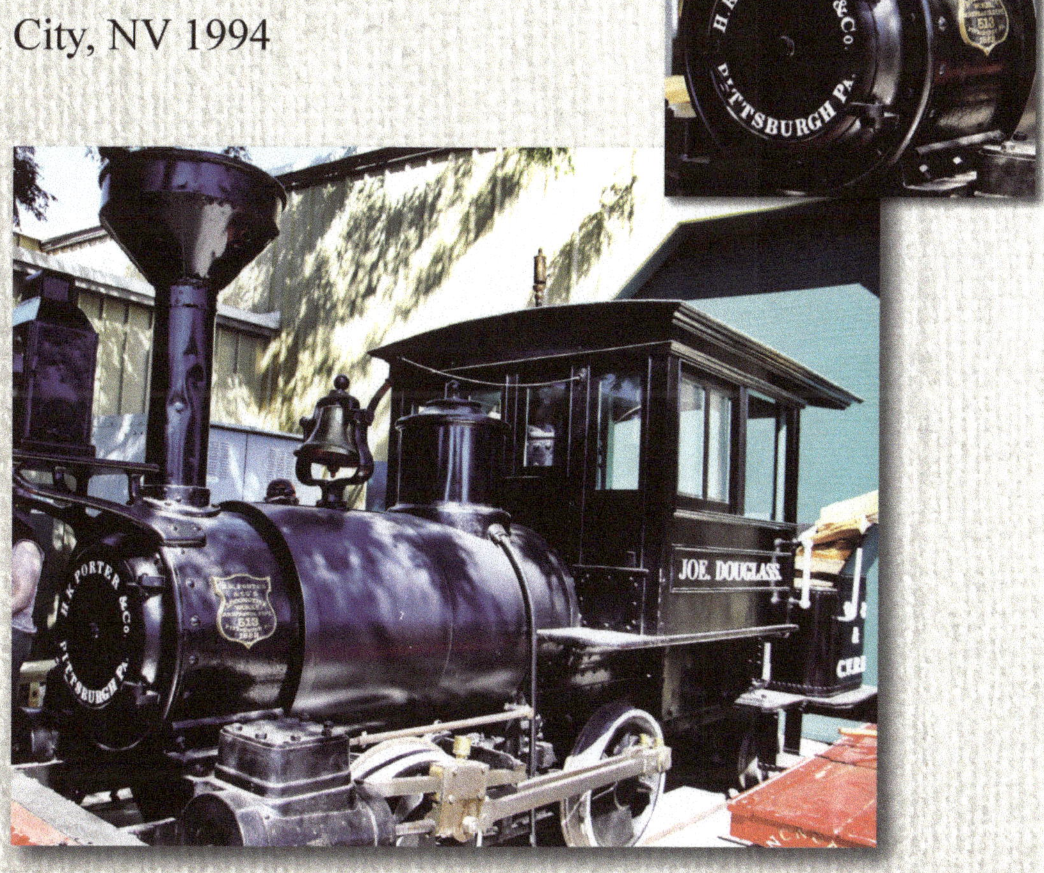

#1 *Antelope and Western*

- 0-4-0T   H. K. Porter, Pittsburgh, PA Builder
- Narrow Gauge
- Built 1889
- On loan at Nevada City, California

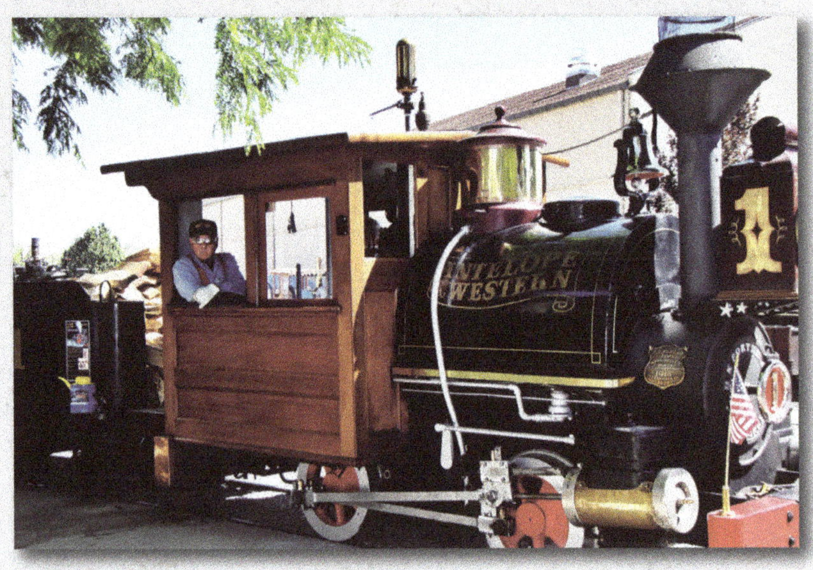
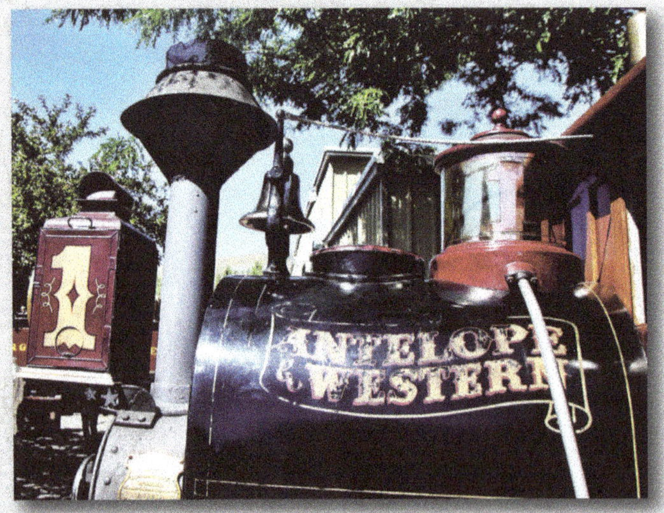

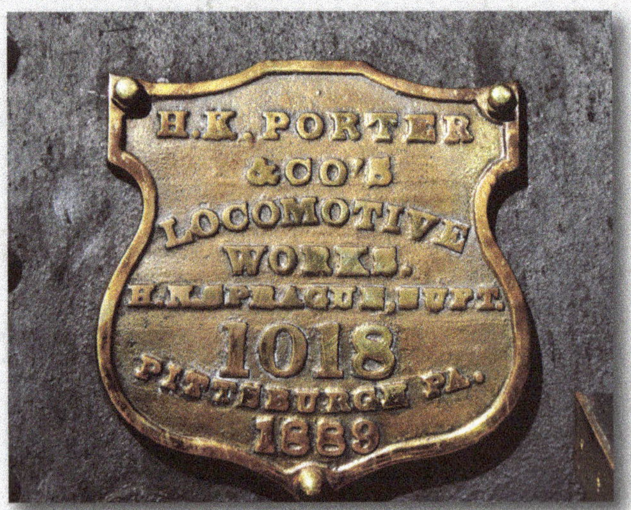

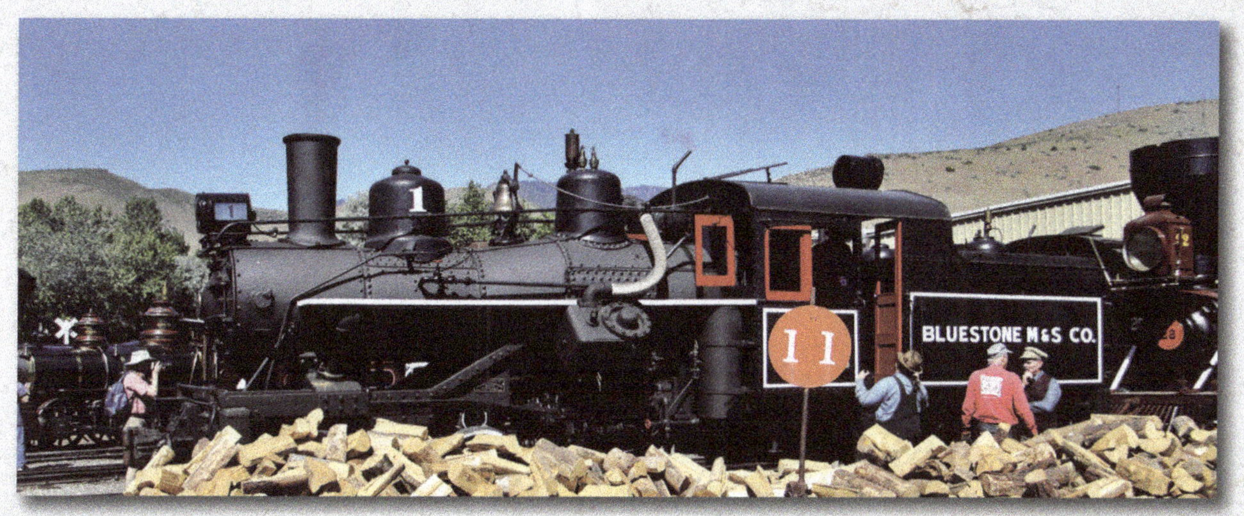

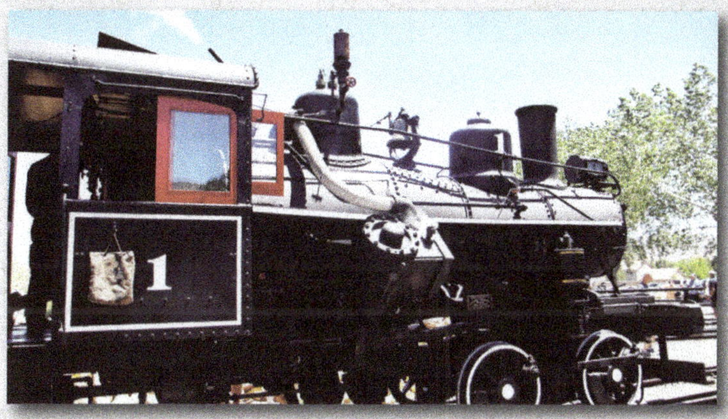

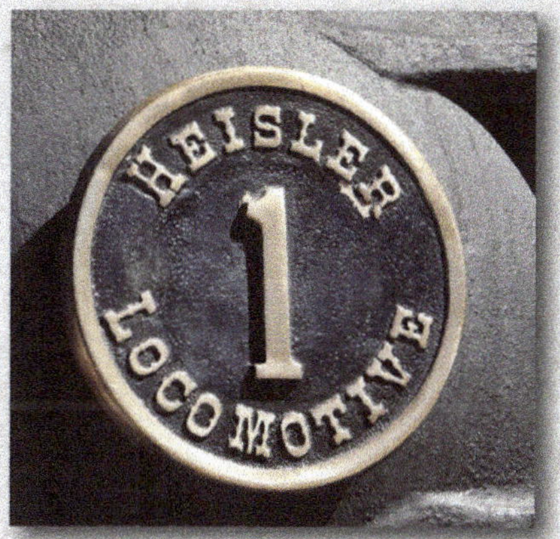

#1 *Bluestone Mining & Smeltering Co. Heisler*

- 4-4-0   Heisler Locomotive Works, Erie, PA Builder
- Narrow Gauge
- Built 1916
- She is now at the Roots of Motive Power Museum, Willits, CA 2006

#2 *Santa Cruz*

- 0-4-0T   H. K. Porter, Pittsburgh, PA Builder
- Narrow Gauge
- Built 1909 Built for the Santa Cruz Portland Cement Co. #2 at Davenport, CA
- Last sold to Efstathios Pappas 2006

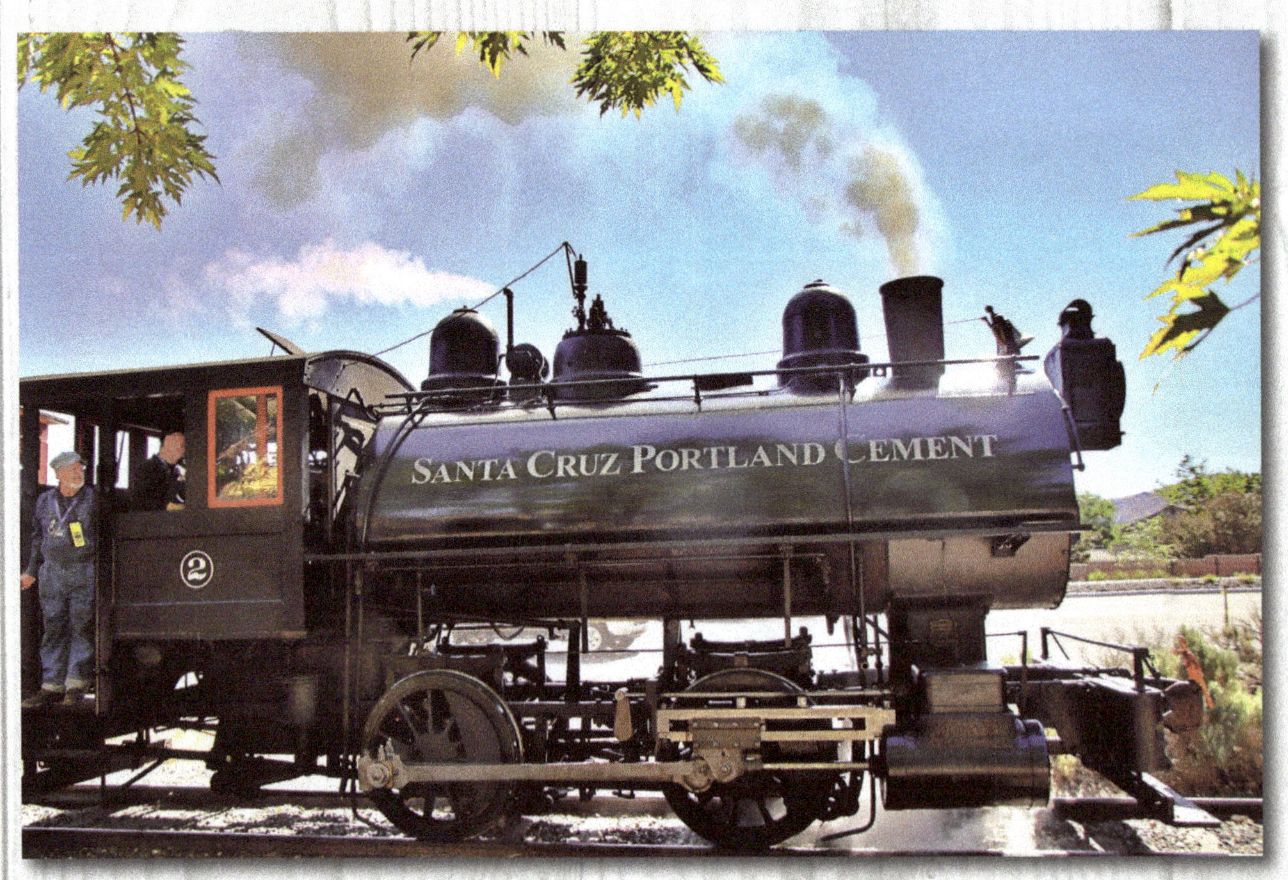

#4 *Eureka*   Eureka and Palisade Railroad

- 4-4-0   Bauldwin Locomotive Works of Philadelphia Builder
- Narrow Gauge
- Built 1875 Retired 1938
- Ran Between Palisade and Eureka, Nevada
- Sold to Warner Brothers Studios 1939
- Sold to Old Vegas Amusement Park 1980
- Sold to attorney Dan Markoff, Las Vegas, Privately stored 1986

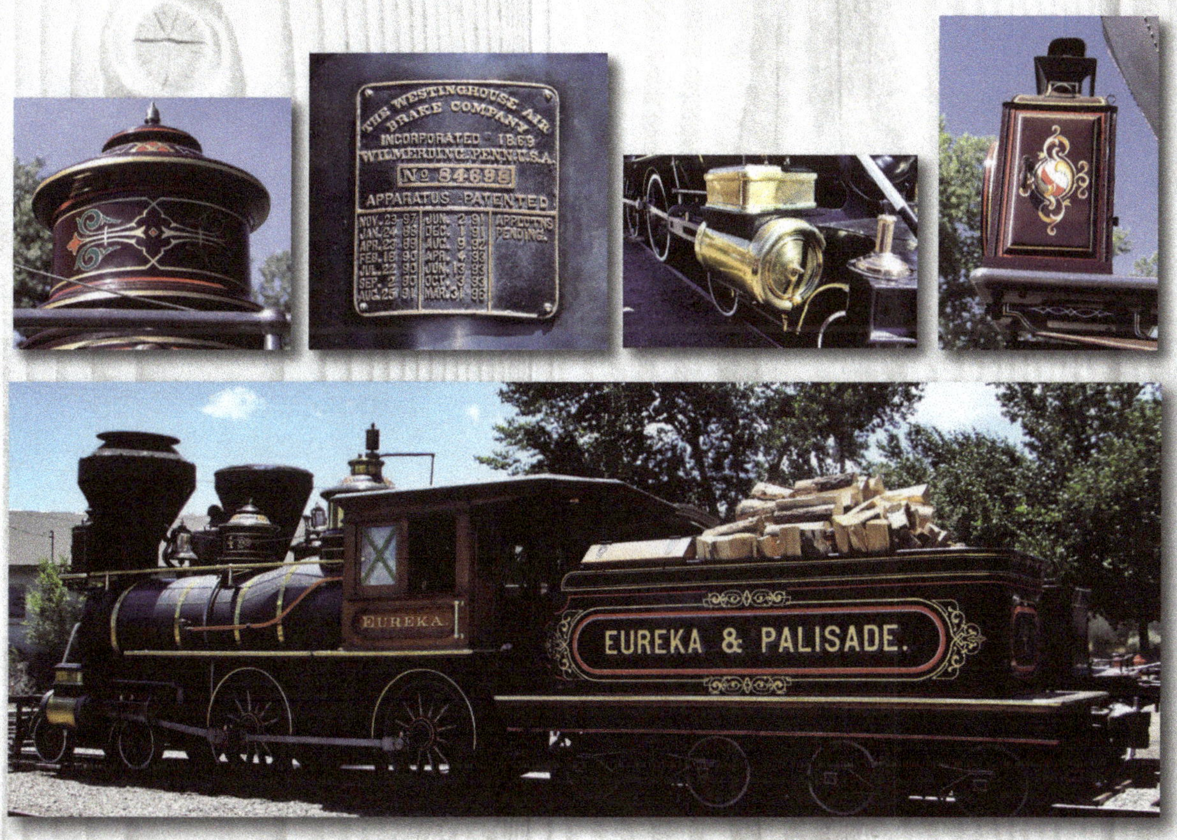

#8 *Dardanelle and Russellville Railroad*

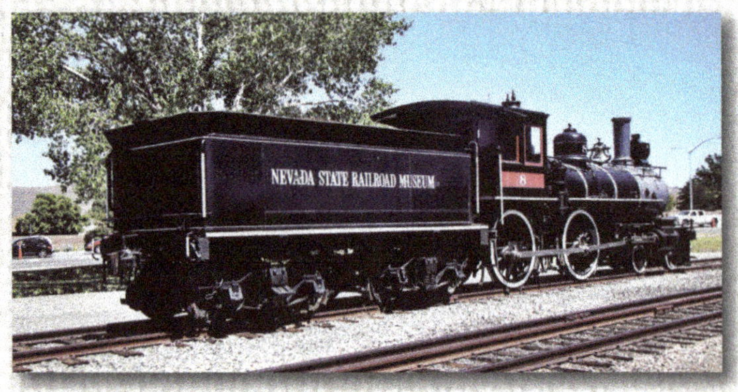

- 4-4-0   Cooke Locomotive and Machine Co., Peterson, NJ Builder
- Standard Gauge
- Built 1888
- Sold to 20th Century Fox 1944
- Moved to Virginia City, NV 1975
- Moved to Nevada State Railroad Museum, Carson City, NV 1989
- In use till 2009

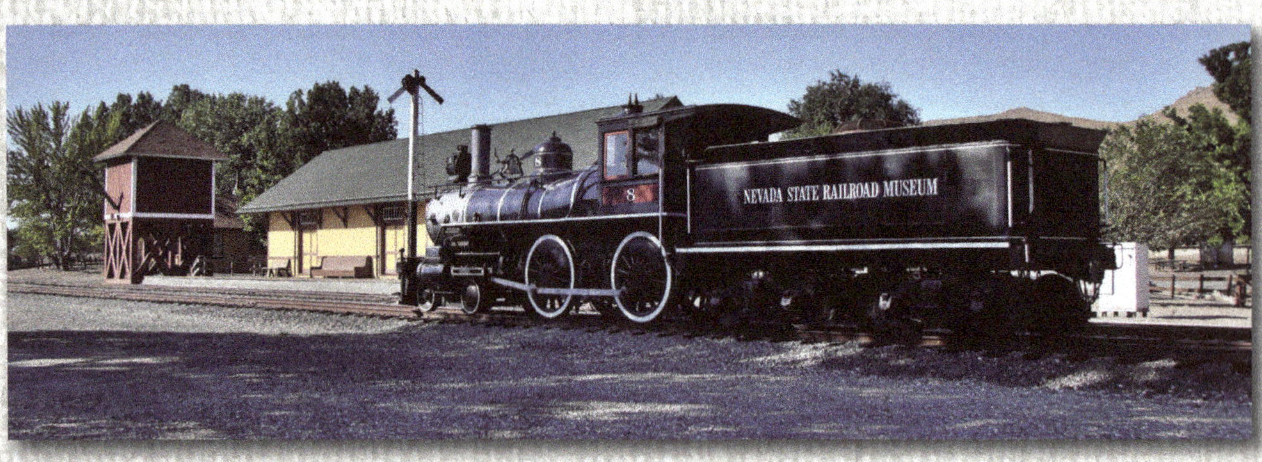

Model T Rail Cars 1923

#23 Roadster Pickup
- Is a kit-based Motor Car from the Western Pacific Railroad and Museum

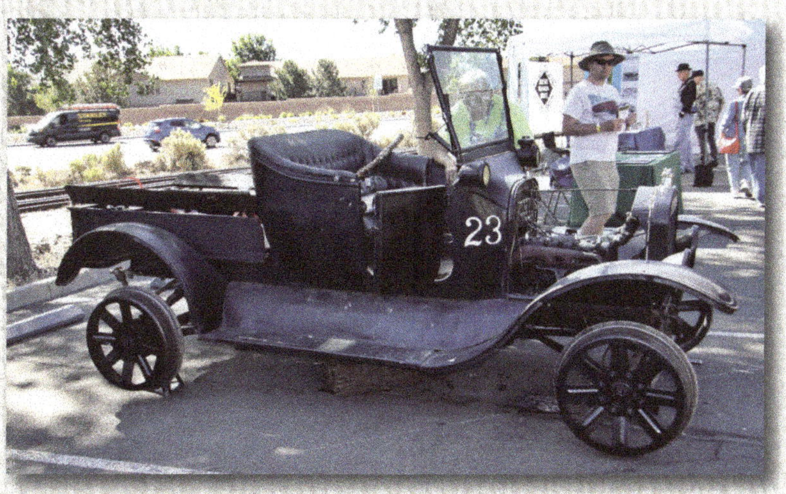

#24 Touring Sedan
- Replica of a car used on the V&T. The original car was wrecked on the V&T in January 1927 in a collision with a freight truck near Browns Station, Reno, NV.

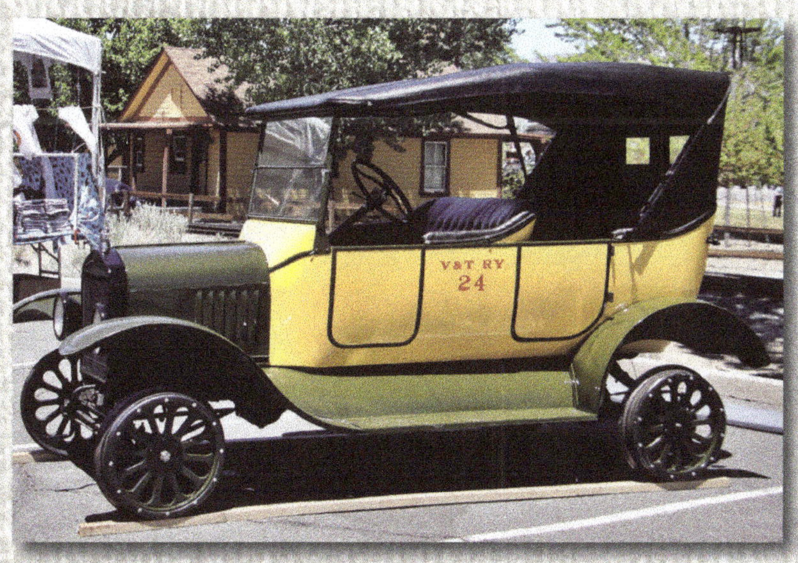

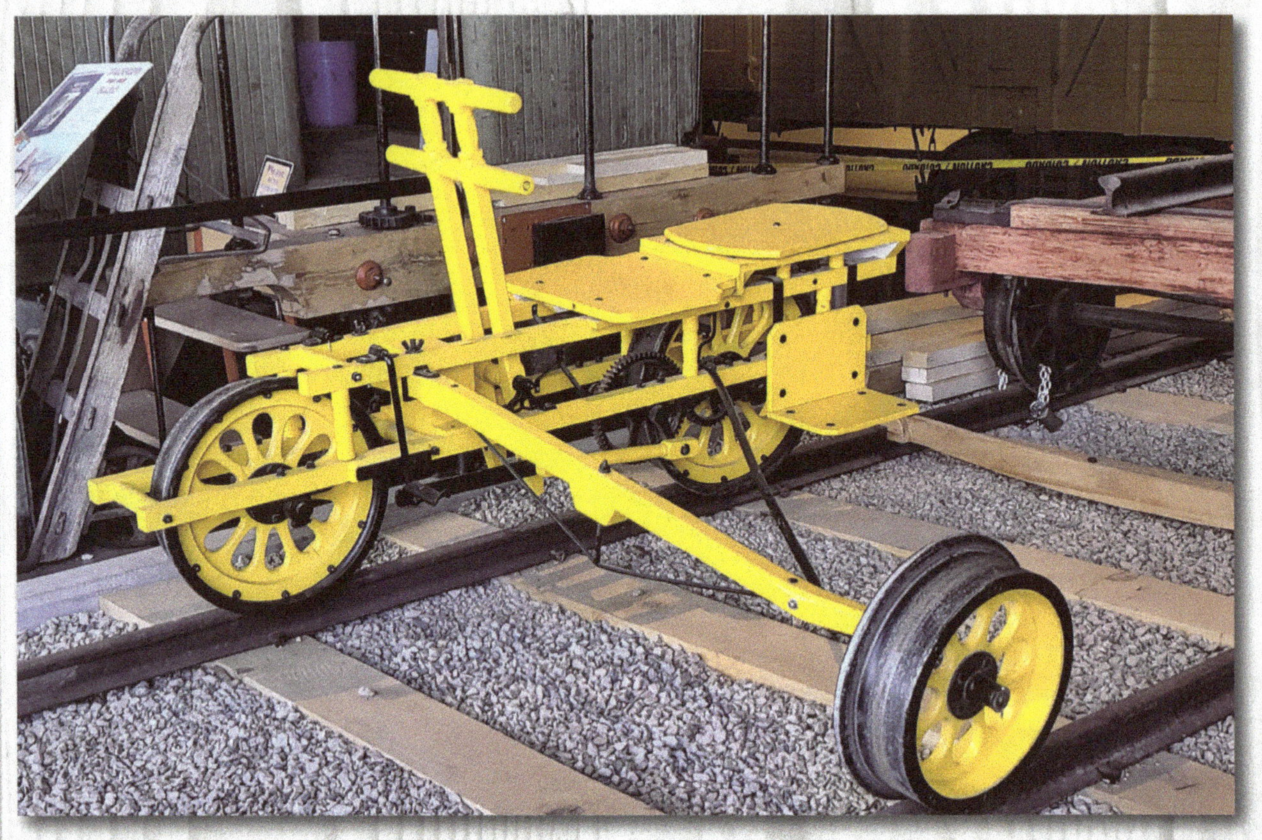

Sheffield Velocipede

- 1879 Three Wheeled Track Car, powered by leg and arm motions
- This velocipede is a reconstruction utilizing the steel and iron parts from a burned velocipede carcass found along the Western Pacific Railroad right-of-way between Reno and Reno Junction, NV.

Miscellaneous Cars

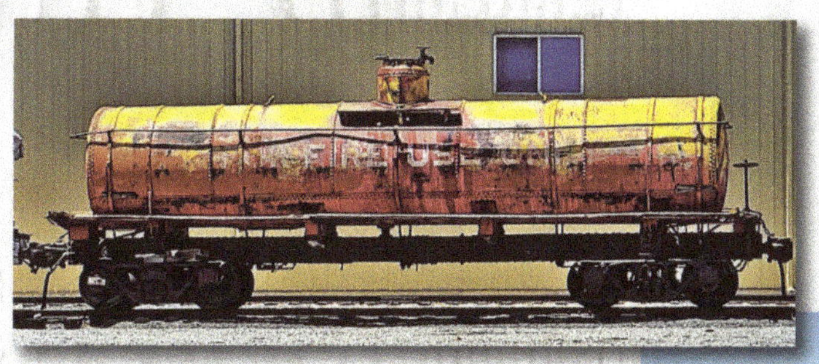

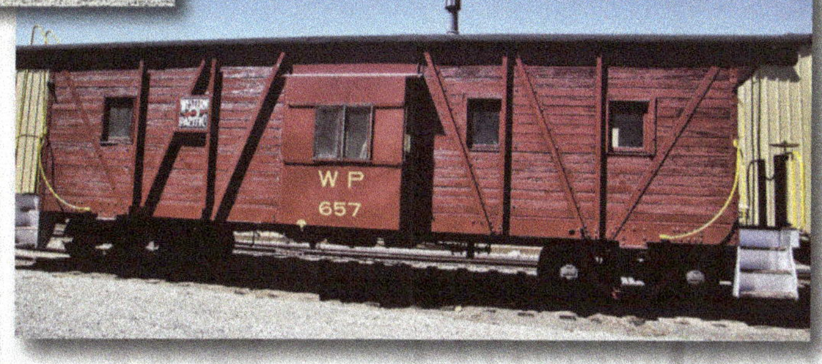

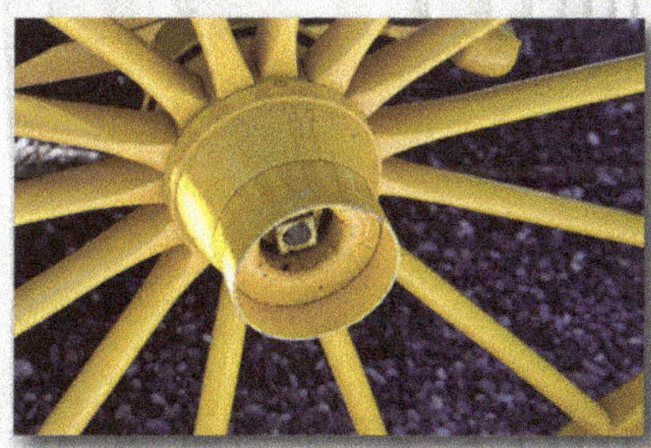

- Carson and Glenbrook U.S.M. (U.S. Mail)

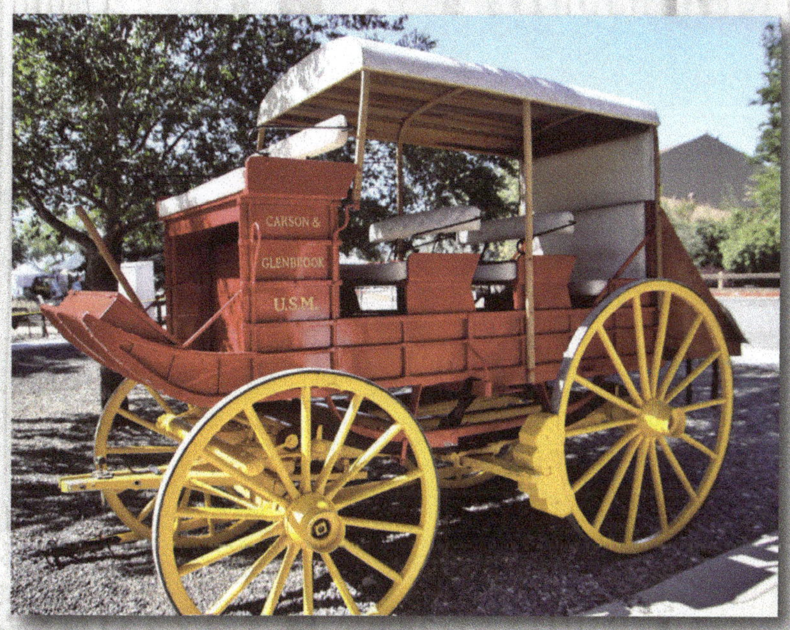

Turn Table

- Built at the Nevada Railroad Museum, Carson City, NV 1985
- Rebuilt 2010

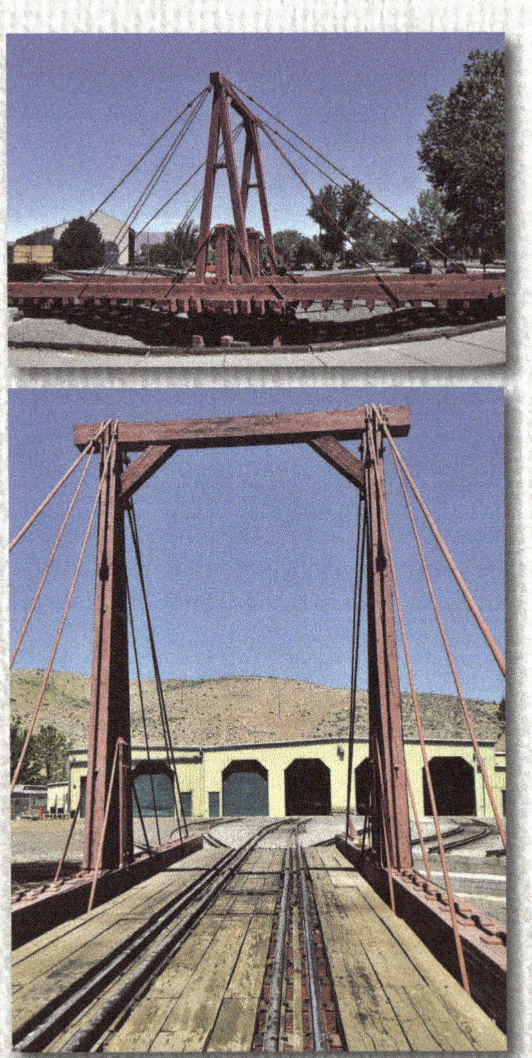

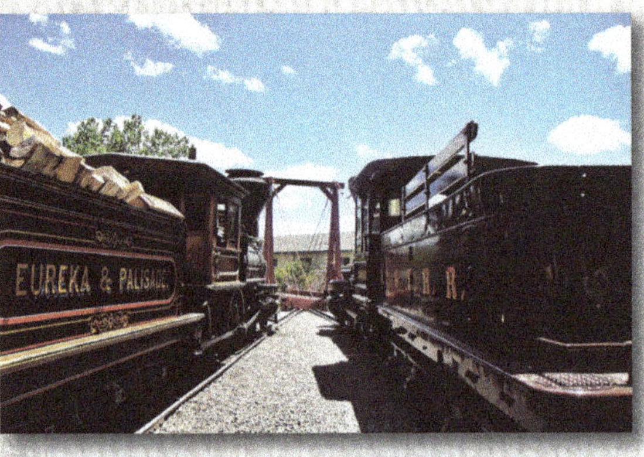

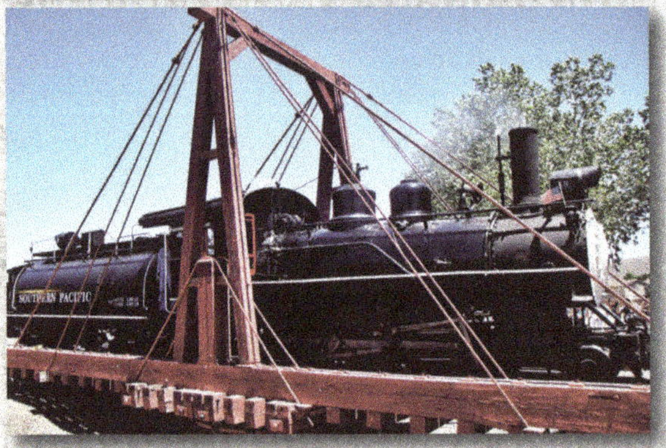

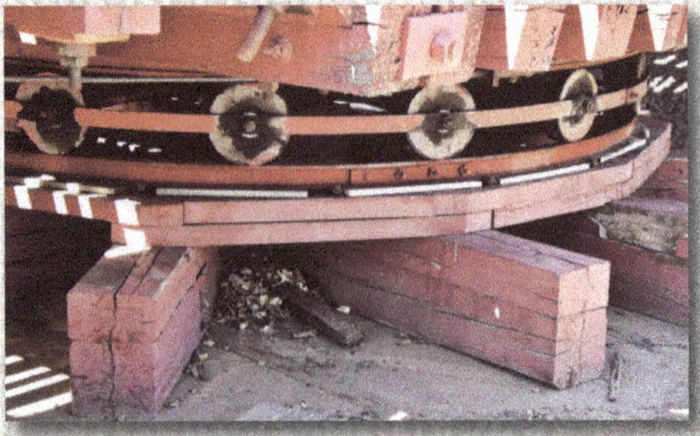

Railroad Parts Boneyard

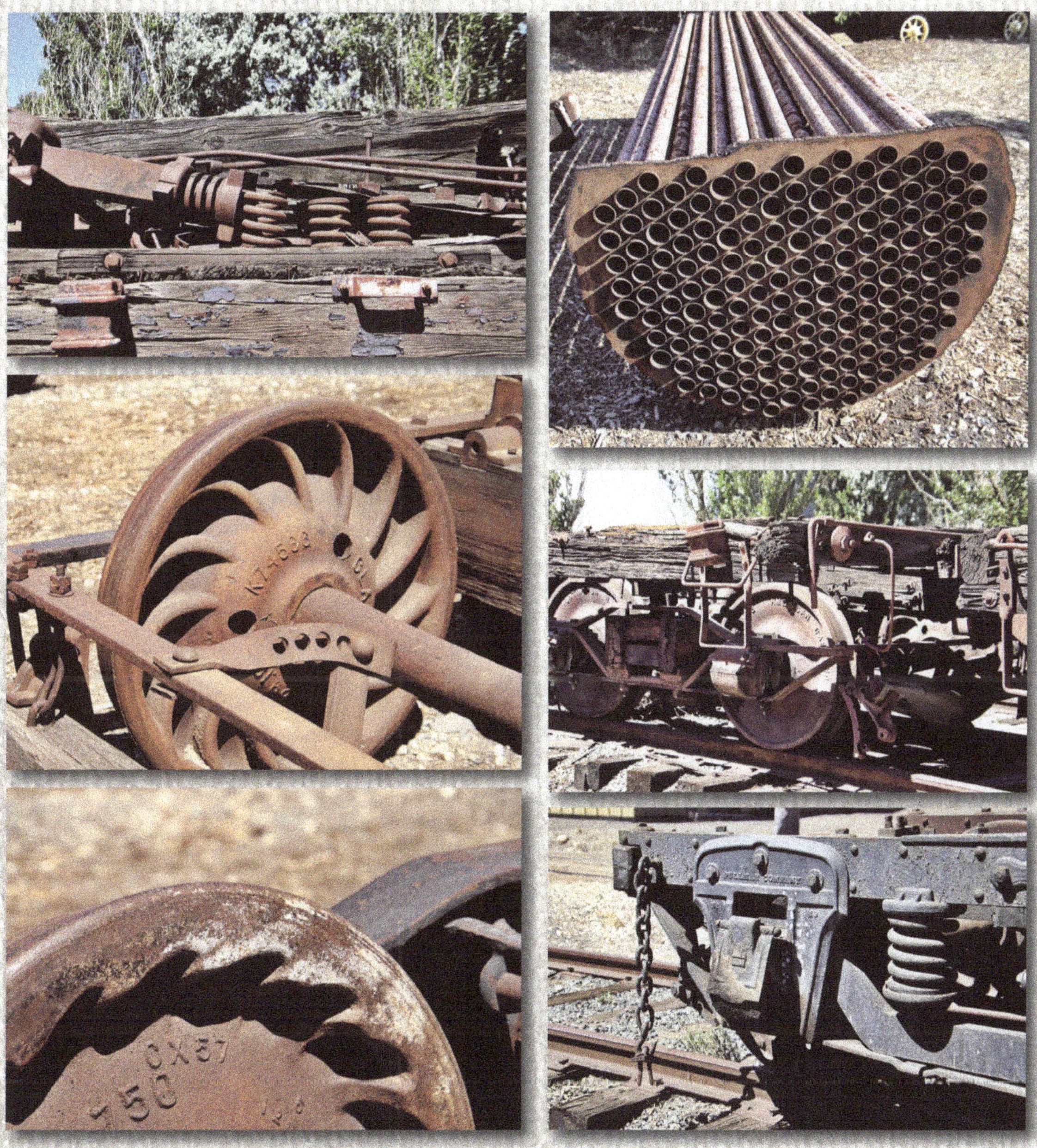

Railroad Cars Boneyard

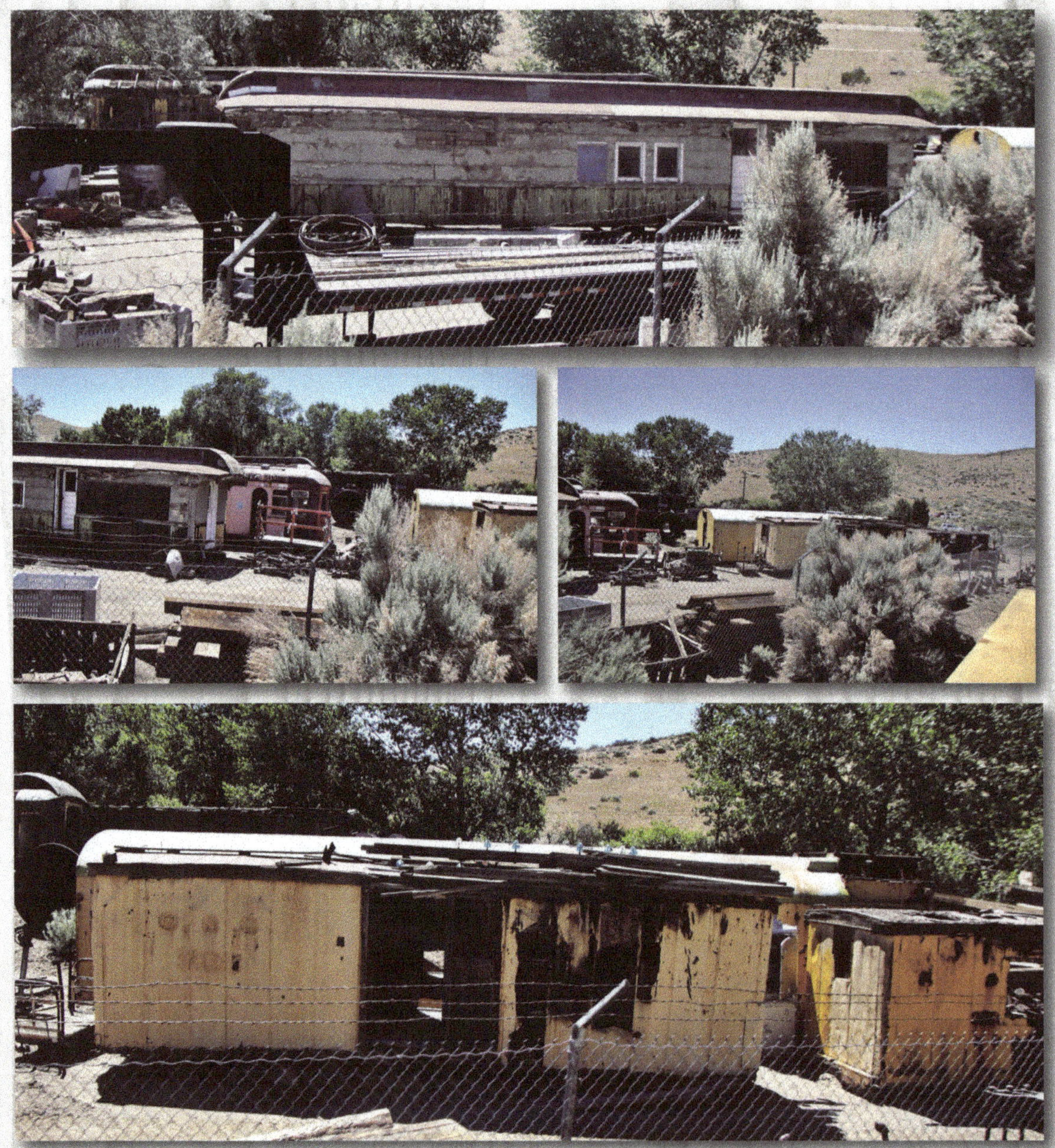

The water tank was built by the Nevada State Railroad Museum at Carson City, NV

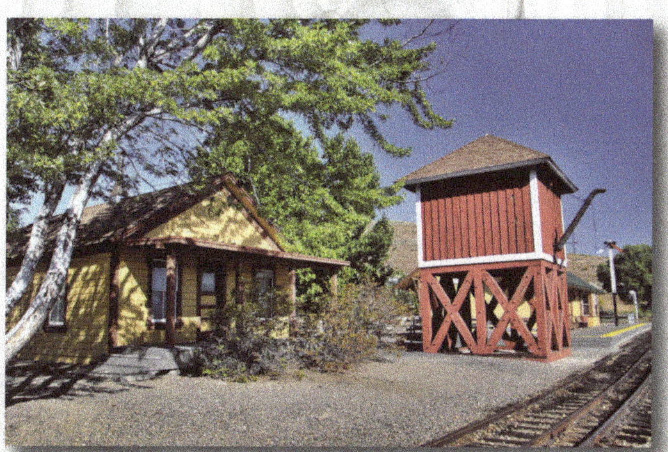

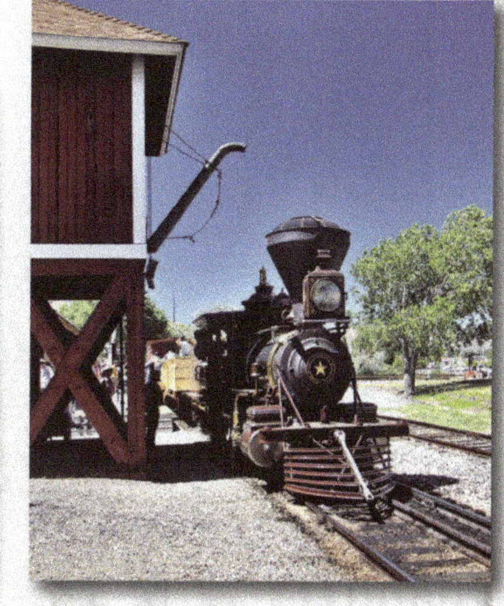

Wabuska Depot was built in 1906 by the Southern Pacific Railroad. It was located between Hazen and Mina, Nevada on the Southern Pacific Line. It remained in service until 1979. SP donated it to the State Railroad Museum at Carson City, NV in 1982. It was relocated in 1984 and restored to its former glory.

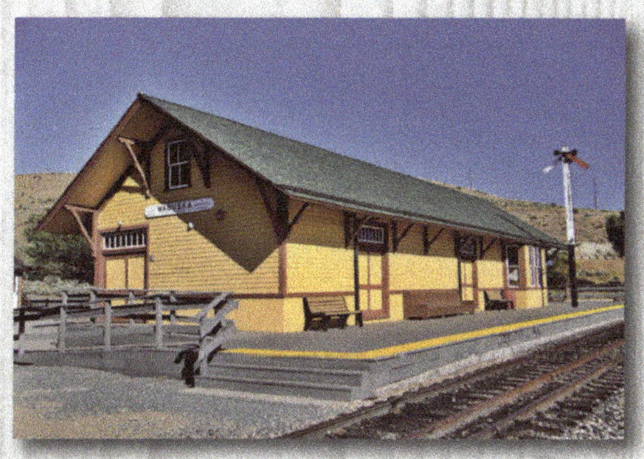

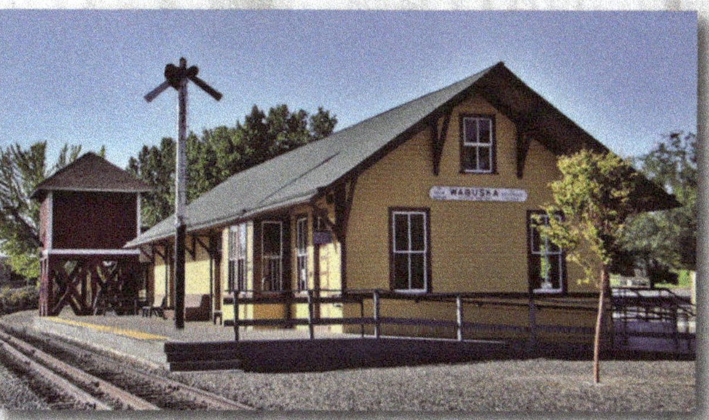

Track Layouts

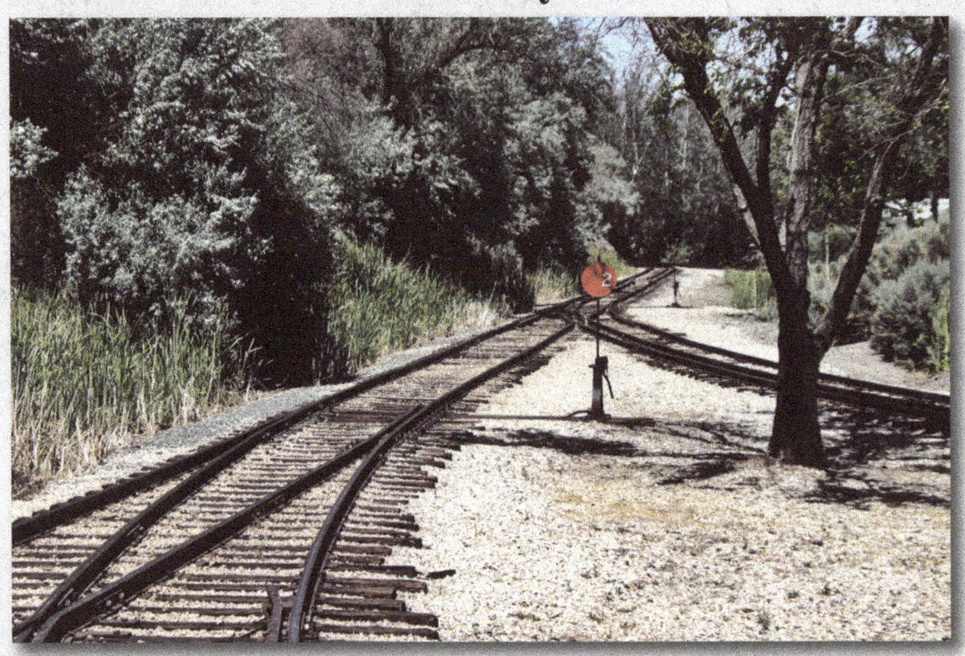

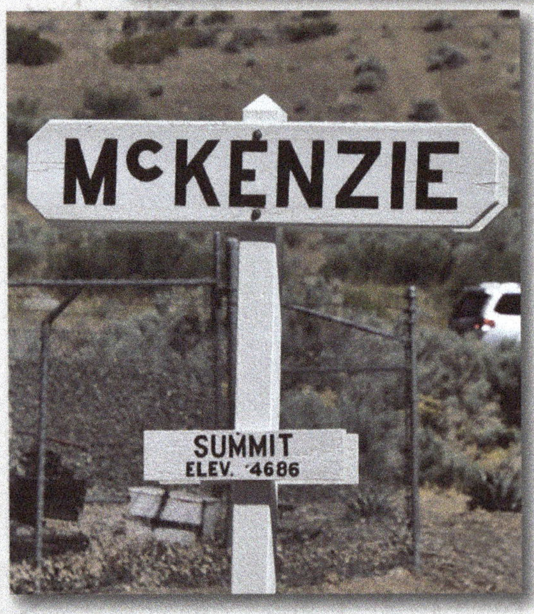

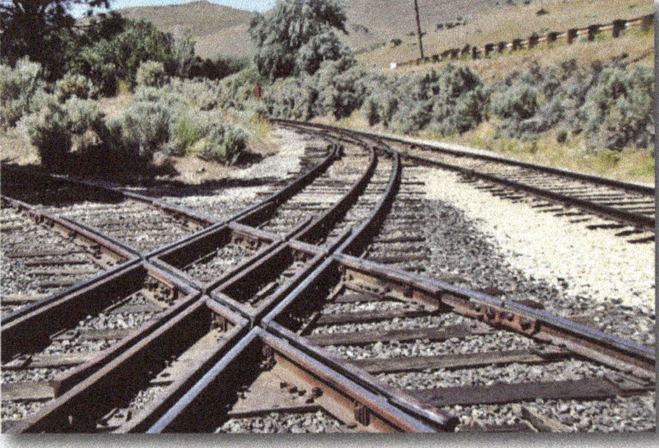

Clapp and Jones Steam Pumper Fire Engine

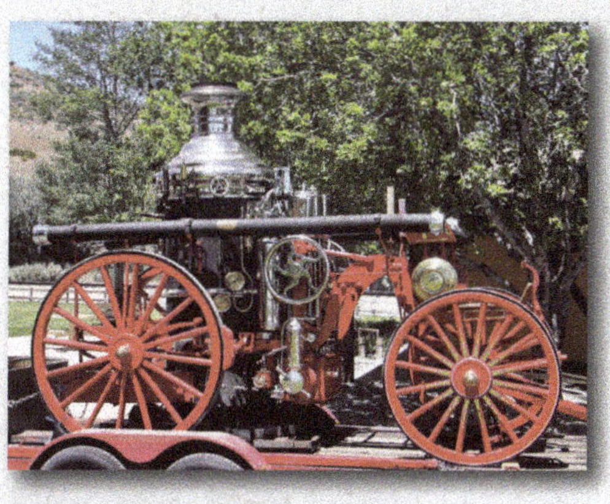

- Built 1879
- Manufactured in Hudson, NY
- Manufacturer's number 313
- It was the property of 20th Century Fox Studios 1945
- Sold at auction 1971
- On loan to Comstock Fireman's Museum, Virginia City, NV 1971
- Now belongs to the Comstock Fireman's Museum

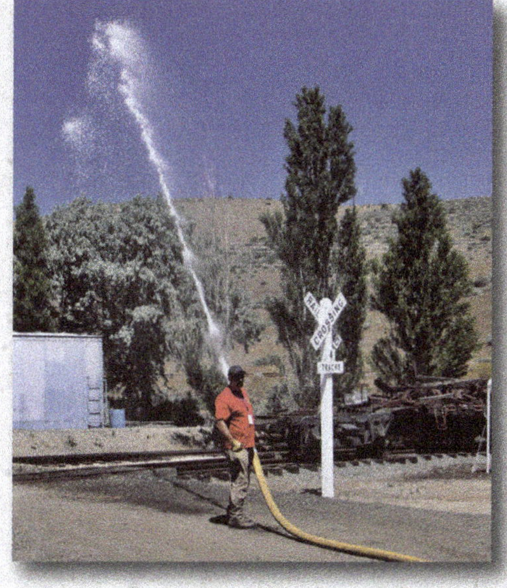

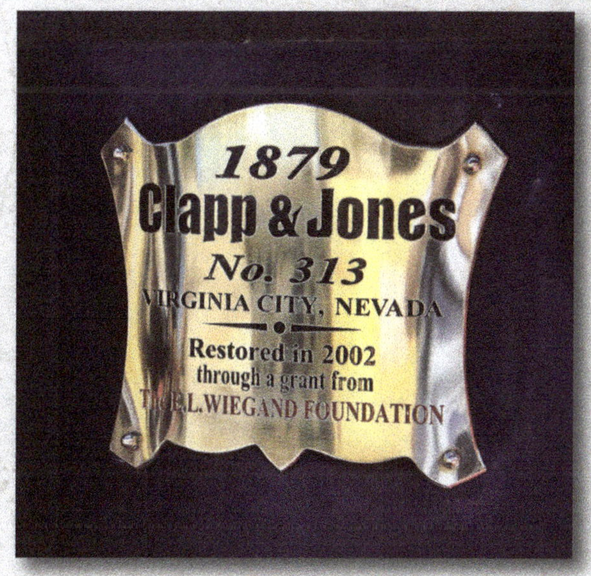